FENG SHUI

for the perfect wedding

FENG SHUI
for the perfect wedding

by Debra Keller
Edited by Kelli F. Giammarco
Illustrated by Mary Ross

ARIEL BOOKS

**Andrews McMeel
Publishing**
Kansas City

FENG SHUI
for the perfect wedding

Never underestimate the influence of a wedding. We don't mean the fact that you arrive single and leave married; we mean the *environment* in which that event occurs. Think of the impact it has on your life! You may only be there for a few blissful (or exhausting) hours, but those are hours you'll remember for a lifetime, and their feeling can affect you deeply and forever. So why not make your wedding as perfect as possible by setting its tone with Feng Shui?

No matter where you get married—a church, a backyard, on the bluffs above the sea, even in the wicker basket of a hot air balloon—you can use wedding Feng Shui to make the space your own and fill it with a loving energy that can affect your marriage for years to come.

Feng Shui is the ancient Chinese art of arranging an environment to influence one's life in a number of positive ways. The words *Feng Shui* literally mean "wind and water"—two of the most vital life-giving elements on

Earth. By applying the principles of Feng Shui to your wedding, you can create a harmonious atmosphere that fortifies love, passion, romance, excitement, and success.

Feng Shui is based on the belief that everything on Earth is teeming with energy (called *chi)* and all energy seeks a state of balance. When active chi (yang) is in balance with passive chi (yin) harmony exists and life could not be better. Love thrives, happiness abounds, good health is abundant, and plenty of opportunities knock.

Some people consider Feng Shui an environmental science because it involves manipulating the physical elements of a space to create a positive psychological effect. Move furniture, add colors and objects, open pathways, enhance light—when you mindfully alter the flow of energy in a space, you can't help but affect how people within it feel.

Though Feng Shui is typically associated with home and office life, it works equally well when applied to weddings and receptions because they're such emotionally significant events. Arrange tables to encourage communication, use colored ribbons to fan the fires of desire, decorate with objects to strengthen your bond. Even the direction you face when you cut the cake can have a profound effect on the destiny of your marriage.

Although there are definite guidelines to Feng Shui, it's largely an intuitive art. To begin, you need only understand its basic principles, then trust yourself to apply them in whatever manner you feel best.

Wedding Feng Shui isn't difficult. All it requires is a little knowledge, a belief in your abilities, and the desire to begin your life together in the most auspicious way.

So sit down with your sweetheart, your mom, your best friend, or alone and flip through the pages of this book. Discover some age-old Feng Shui beliefs as well as practical suggestions for a modern wedding. Use them, too, as a springboard for your own intuition in creating the wedding—and the marriage—of your dreams.

WEDDING GOWN CHI

Vintage (or gently used) wedding gowns carry a trace of their previous owner's chi. This isn't a problem if you know and love the bride who wore it before you. But if you don't, be sure to purify its chi before your wedding. Pass a ringing bell over the gown several times, or leave it overnight next to a bowl of sea salt to banish any negative chi that might affect your marriage.

SOMETHING BLUE

It's a great idea to wear something blue at your wedding, but not because Western tradition holds that you should. Blue is the Feng Shui color of peace and serenity—two qualities a typical bride could use more of!

FABRIC CHI

When selecting your wedding gown, bridesmaid dresses, ushers' suits, and groom's tuxedo, consider the fabric carefully. Each type of fabric carries its own kind of chi that can affect the energy of its wearer. Textured fabrics (linen, raw silk, brocade) are typically yin and carry a quiet energy, while smooth fabrics (polyester, silk, satin) tend to be yang and are filled with excitement. The most harmonious wedding parties are those dressed in a variety of fabrics carefully chosen to create a balance of chi.

BLACK AND WHITE

When it comes to traditional black-and white-weddings, there's more there than meets the eye. The color scheme may be historically Western, but its energy would please any Feng Shui master. Black and white are a perfect balance of yin and yang and offer an ideal start to a harmonious life together.

THINGS THAT ENHANCE ROMANCE

You can never have too much romance at a wedding. Here are some ways to add more to yours:

- **Color:** Use red and purple . . . a lot! These are the Feng Shui colors of romance and passion. Use them in flower arrangements, sashes and bows, candles, bridesmaid's dresses . . . even your bridal gown.

- **Pairs:** Two of anything increases romance, because pairs symbolize relationships. If you have one of something, add another.

- **Fire:** Fire energy is the most passionate. To raise the romantic temperature of your wedding, light candles or get married among palm trees.

WHEN IN DOUBT

If on the day of your wedding you awake with cold feet, place a small bowl of rice near your altar. Rice is said to absorb negative energy (as well as doubt) while attracting good luck and fortune.

THE LIGHTNESS OF BEING

Light brings energy into a space and emotional lightness to a marriage. Choose well-lit rooms for an indoor wedding. Look for those with plenty of windows, or lamps that cast light upward so it's reflected back down (like sunlight). But fear not if you fall in love with someplace dark—mirrors double whatever light there is.

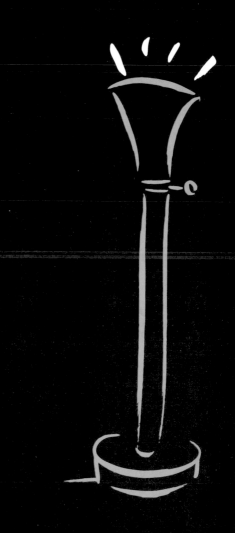

THREE DIRECTIONS

If your wedding will take place in a small part of a larger environment (a room in a hotel, a corner of a park, a chapel on a religious campus) consider its location carefully. The three most auspicious locations for getting married are in the southeast, southwest, or west. All three enhance harmony, homemaking, and contentment.

CHAIR CHI

If you're required to arrange your own ceremony seating, you'd be wise to position both chairs and rows with ample room between them. Not only will your guests appreciate the extra leg room and elbow space, but it will allow for a more positive flow of chi—two things that will increase everyone's pleasure.

INVITING FERTILITY

If you want to have children right away, tuck in a fertility symbol southwest (the direction of family) of your altar. Not surprisingly, the most potent fertility symbol is a rabbit. Even better would be a real bunny—but not the Playboy kind.

CENTER SPACE

The center of the space in which you get married is the heart of your new life together. And because the center of any space affects all energies around it— love, luck, family, success, wisdom, wealth, and relationships—it can influence your marriage for years to come. To ensure your marriage is long and fulfilling, place a romantic object as near to the middle of your wedding site as possible. Try rose quartz, a heart-shaped crystal, red flowers, a pair of anything, a photo of the two of you, or a sentimental memento.

SLOPING CEILINGS

Sloping ceilings, like those of many churches and chapels, create a down draft of chi that can leave you feeling overwhelmed. To lift chi and lighten spirits, surround your altar with height—indoor trees, tall plants, a canopy, a trellis, ornamental pillars, floor-lamp-sized candle holders. Anything that draws your eye (and energy) upward will do.

RING IN THE NEW

To ensure the energy of your wedding site is all your own (and thus positive, excited, optimistic!) refresh its chi an hour or so before the ceremony. Ring a bell, tap a gong, dangle wind chimes, gently clap a pair of cymbals—any reverberating sound that pleases you can purify and renew chi.

THE FOUNDATION OF SUCCESS

One way to help ensure a successful marriage is to lay a strong foundation at your wedding. Wrap a clay brick (symbolizing the strength of the earth) in a black cloth (the color of commitment) and place it in the west (the direction of romance) before you say your vows.

THE CHI OF PILLARS

A room with pillars can be a double-edged sword. On the one hand, pillars restrict the flow of chi, like boulders in the path of a stream. On the other hand, they're filled with invigorating tree energy that can lift chi and infuse a room with life. If you end up renting a room with pillars, dress them in flowers and vines (real or artificial) to strengthen their tree energy—and make your reception a whole lot more lively.

CEILING BEAMS

Beware of altars under ceiling beams,
which tend to thrust chi downward,
thus upsetting the peacefulness of
anyone below. If you plan to say your
vows in a room with ceiling beams,
be sure to stand between them.

RESTROOM CHI

When shopping for wedding or reception sites, be sure to check out the restrooms. Give high marks to those with a small foyer or double set of doors. The more barriers between newlyweds and toilets the better—they help keep the auspicious chi of a new marriage from going down the drain.

MIRROR, MIRROR

In Feng Shui, mirrors signify abundance. To ensure you have an abundance of love in your marriage, include at least one mirror at your wedding. It can be as conspicuous as a gilded mirror hanging on a wall, or as discreet as a silver vase holding a flower arrangement. Even better would be to position the mirror so it reflects you and your partner at a moment of romantic intensity—when you recite your vows, when you seal your marriage with a kiss, when you cut the cake, or when your arms are entwined during your first dance.

BRANCHING OUT

Branches are an auspicious symbol to have at a
wedding because they can represent the unity of
earthly elements. A typical branch is made of wood,
is tall like fire, is filled with minerals, grows from the
soil, and is nourished with water. They look terrific in
floral arrangements—consider curly willow, pussy
willow, flowering quince, and almond.

BRANCHING UP

Sweeping floral arrangements with long, arching branches not only look gorgeous but can infuse a wedding with energy—as long as nothing droops. Drooping branches (or grass leaves) aim tree chi downward and can inhibit your growth as a couple. Make sure all branch tips point up, even if the angle is slight.

PAINTING WITH RIBBONS

The psychology of color is basic to Feng Shui, but you can't paint a rented room—so paint your wedding with ribbons instead! Tie them to pew aisles, chair backs, centerpieces, bouquets, napkin rings, place cards, vases, table legs—anywhere they're visible enough to affect the energy of those within. Here are a few suggestions on how to paint a mood:

- Red promotes romance. Fiery red can create an atmosphere of love. In pink shades, it inspires playfulness—a great color for around the dance floor.

- Orange inspires warmth. It's especially useful in encouraging meaningful communication. Use lots of orange if yours is a second marriage.

- Yellow encourages cheerfulness. It can lighten dark areas and even brighten night receptions. Pale yellow and ecru are terrific for winter ceremonies.

- Green promotes excitement. Its vibrant energy is stimulating and optimistic—an auspicious choice for young couples or those eager to start a family.

- Blue inspires harmony. It also encourages calm. It's an ideal color for whenever children are part of the event, like on a flower girl basket or a ring bearer pillow.

- Violet encourages passion. It's a great choice for sexy evening weddings. But because it also can inspire social success, it's beneficial at receptions with formal seating arrangements.

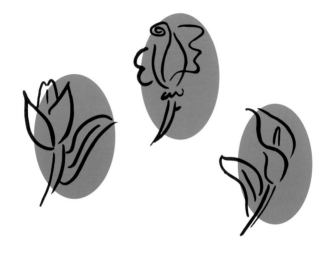

THE CHI OF FLOWERS

The shape, scent, and color of flowers affect chi in different ways. Here are a few flowers to consider when creating your bridal bouquet:

- **tulip**—increases ambition
- **cosmos**—promotes family harmony
- **ranunculus**—attracts wealth
- **flowering quince**—creates opportunity
- **snapdragon**—bolsters spirituality
- **sweet pea**—enhances creativity
- **rose**—invites romance
- **lily**—increases sensuality
- **ivy**—enhances vitality

EIGHT DIRECTIONS

In Feng Shui terms, the most auspicious shaped room is an octagon—its eight walls allow for a flow of chi that fosters all types of love, harmony, and success. If your wedding or reception site is a four-sided room, you can change its energy into that of an octagon by placing a small mirror or tall plant in each of the four corners.

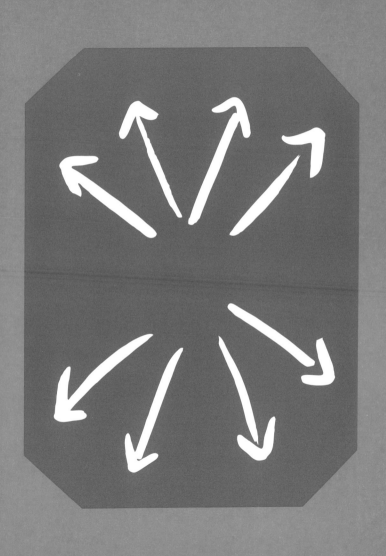

THE FIVE ELEMENTS

According to the ancient principles of Feng Shui, the five earthly elements are a union in perfect harmony. To ensure your marriage is also harmonious, include a symbol of each element at your wedding. Here are a few to consider:

- **Tree (life) symbols:** baskets, branches, plants, wood, paper, anything green

- **Fire (passion) symbols:** candles, mirrors, wall sconces, a fireplace, anything red

- **Soil (security) symbols:** clay pots, stones or pebbles, soil or sand, anything brown

- **Metal (strength) symbols:** candlesticks, utensils, picture frames, anything white

- **Water (serenity) symbols:** vases, fountains, real ponds or streams, anything black

Once upon a time rice was tossed at newlyweds as a means of casting wishes for fertility. While rice is still an important Feng Shui symbol of happiness, it's no longer in vogue at Western weddings. Instead of rice, consider tossing the following:

- **birdseed**—its soil energy can infuse a marriage with comfort

- **bubbles**—filled with water energy, it's said they can impart peace

- **flower petals**—their lively tree energy can help a marriage stay fresh

- **confetti**—its strong metal energy can help a marriage grow rock solid

- **sequins**—their fiery energy can fan the flames of passion

QUESTION

In which direction should a just-married couple walk down the aisle?

ANSWER

East—the direction of new beginnings, happiness, and the realization of dreams.

If you want your wedding to be fairy-tale perfect, pay close attention to seating at your reception. Use the chart below to balance personality traits and ensure harmony all around.

- Sitting north, facing south—encourages social interaction. Best for people who are shy.

- Sitting northeast, facing southwest—promotes family harmony. Good for family members and future in-laws.

- Sitting east, facing west—enhances pleasure and contentment. Good for complainers.

- Sitting south, facing northwest—encourages listening. Good for people who talk too much.

- Sitting south, facing north—promotes tranquillity. Best for overbearing personalities.

- Sitting southwest, facing northeast—enhances patience. Best for children and people who tend to get restless.

- Sitting west, facing east—encourages activity. Best for older people or people with physical disabilities.

- Sitting northwest, facing southeast—promotes communication. Best for teenagers and young adults.

SETTING THE MOOD

The colors of table linens can have a profound influence on the mood of a room. Set the mood of your reception when you set your tables by choosing your colors wisely.

- Red for romance
- Orange for harmony
- Yellow for warmth
- Green for activity
- Blue for communication
- Purple for passion
- Brown for practicality
- White for excitement
- Gray for dignity
- Beige for relaxation
- Pink for playfulness
- Black for security

AUSPICIOUS TABLES

The most auspicious tables for wedding receptions are those that are round. Round tables draw guests together and invite lively conversation.

TABLE CONFETTI

An easy way to affect the mood of your reception is to sprinkle each table with confetti. It works as well at formal weddings as it does at casual buffets. The trick is to choose a type of confetti whose energy creates the mood you desire. Here are a few choices to consider:

- Rose petals encourage love and create an atmosphere of romance.

- Orange peels uplift chi and infuse a room with luck.

- Sequins support a creative environment where self-expression is welcome.

- Traditional paper confetti fosters an atmosphere of acceptance and harmony.

- Leaves stimulate chi and invite friendships to bloom.

- Glass beads or crystals encourage understanding and heighten spirituality.

- Pebbles lend an environment strength and support.

- Rice refreshes a room's chi and encourages good health.

MORE CHAIR CHI

If you can choose any type of chair for your reception, choose those that are cloth-covered or made of pale wood. Fabric-covered and softwood chairs are the most yin (calm) and offer an ideal point of balance to a naturally yang (exciting) event, like a wedding.

THE YIN AND YANG OF GLASSES

You have a choice when it comes to choosing champagne glasses: tall, thin flutes that vibrate with yang passion, or low-rimmed glasses that are quietly and romantically yin. You'd be wise to choose those that are opposite of how you'd characterize your relationship to ensure a well balanced and harmonious life together.

QUESTION

In which direction should the best man face when giving his traditional toast?

ANSWER

Southeast—the direction of harmony, communication, and growth.

QUESTION

In which direction should the father of the bride face when making his traditional toast?

ANSWER

Southwest—the direction of family harmony, parenthood, and financial wisdom.

NO CLOCKS

Make sure there are no visible clocks at your reception. The union of love should be timeless.

THE IMPORTANCE OF A WELL-BALANCED MEAL

A well-balanced meal is vital to good health and an overall feeling of well-being. Forget the FDA food pyramid—this is about the yin and yang of foods. Regardless of whether you're planning a sit-down meal, casual buffet, or serving only hors d'oeuvres at your wedding, you should offer your guests a balance of choices.

- Yang foods include smoked salmon, poached or grilled fish, prime rib, chicken, turkey, steak, sausages, lamb, veal, eggs, pasta, rice, whole grain breads, potato salad, carrot salad, and root vegetables.

- Yin foods include leafy salads, leafy vegetables, tofu, legumes, bean salads, nuts, fresh fruit, fruit salads, white breads, soups, gravies, sauces, dressings, beverages, butter, cream, sweeteners, and dessert.

Next to the bride, the wedding cake is the focal point of most receptions. In Feng Shui terms it's a potent symbol of the sweet years to come and can set the tone of a marriage. Here are the four most important aspects to consider when selecting your wedding cake:

- **Height:** Tall cakes are best for outdoor weddings—they symbolize tree energy and represent marital growth. Try to avoid tall cakes in rooms with low ceilings or your optimism may be repressed.

- **Tiers:** Three is the Feng Shui number of love. A three-tiered wedding cake is the most auspicious.

- **Shape:** Round or square (yang) cakes infuse a new marriage with a rush of excitement and energy. Rectangular (yin) cakes begin a marriage on a quiet, romantic note.

- **Color:** The color of your cake should harmonize with the colors of your reception site (not your wedding party) to bring balance to your marriage. The exception is white, which harmonizes with everything. If you want a white wedding cake, color it with flowers, ribbons, confections, or leaves.

QUESTION

In which direction should the newlyweds face when cutting the wedding cake?

ANSWER

Northwest— the direction of responsibility, wisdom, and respect.

QUESTION

In which area of the reception should the wedding cake be?

ANSWER

Southwest—the direction of deepening relationships, family harmony, and continual progress.

QUESTION

In which direction should a bride toss her bouquet?

ANSWER

West—the direction of romance. An auspicious bonus: The anxious maidens facing the bride will be looking east, the direction of new beginnings.

QUESTION

In which direction should a groom toss his bride's garter?

ANSWER

South—the direction of passion and an exciting social life.

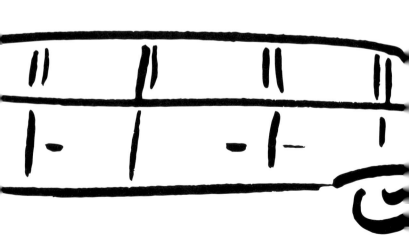

Traveling from your wedding to your reception, honey-moon suite, or home is an important first step in your life journey as a couple. To prepare a rented limo (or horse-drawn carriage or vintage car or pair of Harleys) for your long and successful marriage, hang a crystal from a mirror to attract positive chi and tie on a red ribbon for luck.

By their nature, hotel rooms have a long history of guests, each one leaving behind a trace of his or her energy. To cleanse your honeymoon suite of all previous chi and start your marriage fresh, bring a Feng Shui first-aid kit with you on your honeymoon. Here's what to pack:

- Sea salt in a white bowl—it wicks negative energy from a room the same way table salt absorbs moisture.

- Nine pieces of dried orange peel—evenly spaced around a room, they will chase away difficult chi.

- Incense—it purifies the air for as long as its scent is present; bring a lot.

- Something blue—it calms and quiets the remaining hyperactive chi of a room used by too many people.

- A bell—it purifies and refreshes the chi of a room; like a marriage, it offers a new start.

QUESTION

What color limo should a bride and groom rent?

ANSWER

Black—the Feng Shui color of security. Black can also help strengthen the ties of love.

SECOND WEDDINGS

The energy at second weddings can be less dynamic than it was the first time around. Increase the vibrancy of second-wedding chi with an abundance of yang things: glass vases, stone sculptures, mirrors, bright paintings, metal furniture, warm colors, circles, and squares.

THE CHI OF BEDS

Whether you've never spent a night together or have been living together for years, getting married puts a whole new spin on your relationship. Make sure your marriage bed is ready for it. Position it carefully—the energy of the direction in which your heads point can affect your entire union.

- **East.** This is the direction of tomorrow. Sleeping this way can infuse both of you with a feeling that anything is possible and everything is good.

- **Southeast.** This is the direction of growth. Sleeping this way can inspire your creativity as a couple and ensure easy communication between you.

- **Southwest.** This is the direction of acceptance. Sleeping this way can bring peace and calm and infuse your relationship with mutual respect.

- **West.** This is the direction of commitment. Sleeping this way can tighten the bonds of love and help you build a foundation for forever.

BETWEEN THE SHEETS

To create a harmonious flow of chi between the sheets, dress your bed in natural fibers, like cotton, silk, and linen. For a really fun time, make them purple.

THE ARITHMETIC OF BLISS

It's said joy is governed by the number seven and the element metal. To ensure your marriage is filled with happiness, keep seven metal objects near you at your wedding. A copper penny, a brass button, a silver chain, a gold ring, an iron ornament, a bronze pendant, and a steel pin are all good choices.

OPPORTUNITY'S KNOCKING

The two of you moving in together offers the perfect opportunity for you to cull through everything you own and discard anything you don't use. When was the last time you wore those shoes? How many pairs of salad tongs do you need? And don't forget to tuck away those photos of ex-lovers! Getting rid of old and unwanted things is a great way to declutter your home, refresh chi, and get your marriage off to a healthy start.

WHEN TWO'S A CROWD

Two of anything (except for the two of you, of course!) constitutes a crowd, and nothing stagnates chi faster than a crowded room. It's vital that when you move in together you toss out as many duplicates as you can. Two toasters? Two sets of encyclopedias? Seventeen lamps? Have a garage sale. Here are a few other things to look out for:

- more blankets and pillows than you'll ever use

- mismatched or excess linens

- extra silverware, cutlery, dishes, pots, or pans

- two copies of the same book, CD, video, or DVD

- electronic equipment you only need one of

- excess tools and tool boxes

- garden tools, hoses, and ladders

- too much furniture

GIFTS YOU DON'T WANT

It's every newlywed's nightmare: what to do with the gifts you don't want without hurting the givers' feelings. According to Feng Shui there's only one option—get rid of it! There's no point in keeping a fondue set if you don't like fondue, no matter how much you love the person who gave it to you. Unwanted gifts only collect dust and clutter a home (the two worst chi inhibitors there are). Far better to return it, sell it, or give it away. After all, the gift wasn't given to you to make your life miserable. It was given as a token of love.

HAPPILY EVER AFTER

Keep love blooming for many years to come with these two little words: fresh flowers. Fresh bouquets are a powerful way to fill your home with positive chi. Better yet, mark each anniversary with a romantic bouquet to renew marital energy and spark passion. What better way to say I'll *always* love you?

THIS BOOK WAS DESIGNED
AND TYPESET IN UNIVERS
BY ANN ZIPKIN OF ANN-DESIGN,
KATONAH, NEW YORK.